MARTIAL ARTS
MASTERS

THE GREATEST TEACHERS, FIGHTERS, AND PERFORMERS

By NGO VINH-HOI

A ROXBURY PARK BOOK

Lowell House
Juvenile
Los Angeles

Dedicated to my grandparents,
who led the way

Acknowledgments

Special thanks to all of the martial artists who helped me
write this book: masters, teachers, and students alike.

Manufactured in the United States of America
10 9 8 7 6 5 4 3 2 1

ISBN: 1-56565-559-1

Library of Congress Cataloging-in-Publication Data is available

Publisher: Jack Artenstein
Associate Publisher, Juvenile Division: Elizabeth D. Amos
Director of Publishing Services: Rena Copperman
Managing Editor: Lindsey Hay
Photo Researcher: Jennifer Schulz
Cover photos: Jackie Chan, *shooting star*
          Bruce Lee, *fotos international*
          Chuck Norris, *Michael Neveux/shooting star*

Roxbury Park is an imprint of Lowell House.

Lowell House books can be purchased at special discounts when
ordered in bulk for premiums and special sales. Contact
Department JH at the following address:
Lowell House Juvenile
2029 Century Park East, Suite 3290
Los Angeles, CA 90067

CONTENTS

INTRODUCTION

What makes a person a martial arts *master*? Skill alone is not sufficient. There are many martial artists who are skilled technicians or extraordinarily tough fighters, yet they have done little to advance their art. Mastery requires a deep dedication to one's art and the desire to further it without fundamentally changing its nature.

All of the people included in this book have in some way furthered the martial arts. Men and women like Dr. Jigoro Kano, Gichin Funakoshi, and Bow Sim Mark were and are great teachers. Performers like Jackie Chan and Bruce Lee deserve inclusion simply because they have done so much in popularizing the martial arts.

The other trait all these people share is perseverance, often in the face of great adversity. There are many equally important and deserving masters, but this small handful exemplifies the combination of skill, discipline, dedication, and passion essential to the survival and prosperity of the martial arts.

MIYAMOTO MUSASHI*
(1584–1645)

Miyamoto Musashi was the greatest swordsman in Japanese history. He was also an effective military leader and a sensitive artist, but he remains best known for his supreme skill with a sword.

His story has become inescapably intertwined with the legends that have grown up around him and his deeds. So it's hard to tell where the truth ends and the myth begins. This is the most commonly agreed-upon account of his life.

Musashi was born to an ancient warrior family in or around 1584. His full name was Shinmen Musashi no Kami Fujiwara no Genshin, but he eventually took the name Miyamoto in honor of his birthplace, Miyamoto village in Mimasaka Province. Musashi was born and raised in an exceptionally tumultuous period of Japanese history. Powerful warrior clans warred against each other constantly, and great noblemen such as Ida Nobunaga, Hideyoshi Toyotomi, Shingen

*Legendary Japanese actor Toshiro Mifune (pictured above) portrayed Musashi in the 1954 epic *Samurai Trilogy*.

STATE OF THE ART

The art of kenjutsu (Japanese swordsmanship) seeks to achieve perfect timing, power, and focus. The goal is to defeat the enemy with a single blow. Musashi took this idea to an extreme, facing many of his opponents armed only with a wooden bokken, even when they used steel katanas.

Even when he used real blades, Musashi refused to be bound by tradition. Usually, a samurai was armed with both a katana and a *wakizashi* (short sword). The paired swords were actually a sign of rank. And only the katana was used in battle. But the innovative Musashi was always seeking to confuse his opponents and often fought with a sword in each hand. His two-weapon method of swordsmanship became known as the *nito-ryu* style.

Takeda, and Ieyasu Tokugawa vied to unite the country and claim the title of shogun. Although in theory Japan was ruled by a divine emperor, for several hundred years true leadership had rested with *shoguns* (military rulers) who ruled in the emperor's name.

Little is known of Musashi's childhood except that he was orphaned at age seven and was raised by his uncle, a Buddhist priest. Musashi grew into a large, strong, and hot-tempered youth who was always spoiling for a fight.

When he was sixteen Musashi decided to leave his home village and make a name for himself as a warrior. He enlisted in the army of Shogun Hideyoshi Toyotomi. Toyotomi's greatest rival was Ieyasu Tokugawa, the craftiest of all the clan leaders, who defeated all his rivals, became shogun, and established a dynasty that would last more than 250 years.

By 1600 Hideyoshi Toyotomi had died, and a nobleman named Mitsunari Ishida was ruling in the name of Toyotomi's infant son, Hideyori. A power vacuum resulted, and the lack of a strong leader pitched Japan into civil war. Ieyasu Tokugawa and his allies fought Ishida and his allies.

Tokugawa was one of the smartest and most ruthless
military leaders the world has ever known. He
forced Ishida into a decisive battle at
Sekigahara. For three days the opposing forces
raged back and forth across the field. When the
fighting was over, more than 70,000 warriors
had been killed. Tokugawa's troops routed
Toyotomi's army, hunting down and
slaughtering the survivors. That's
the way such wars were fought
then—no mercy. The only reason
Musashi survived was because he
hid from the Tokugawa patrols for
days and escaped by crawl-
ing among the corpses
of his comrades, lap-
ping water from
muddy puddles when
he was overcome with
thirst.

With the war behind
him, Musashi set out to
perfect his fighting skills.
He roamed all over Japan
for nearly a decade, fighting more than sixty duels.

Sometimes Musashi even had
to face whole *kenjutsu* (swordsmanship) schools, but he
always prevailed, striking
down all of his foes. As
Musashi sought greater challenges for his skill, he would
often use a *bokken* (a wooden practice sword) in his
matches, even against opponents armed with razor-sharp
katana (the traditional long steel sword of a samurai).

During this period Musashi began to develop a reputation as a real oddball. In contrast to the typical well-
groomed samurai, his appearance was wild and unkempt.

7

He would often sleep in caves or other places in the wild rather than seeking the comfort of an inn during his travels. He was a master strategist, and his fierce demeanor and bizarre behavior may have been carefully calculated to frighten and confuse his rivals.

DID YOU KNOW?

For many years Musashi refused to take a bath for fear that he would be ambushed. His fears aside, his wretched personal hygiene must have been enough to keep away most enemies.

Legend has it that Musashi's final duel occurred in 1612 on Ganryu Island, off the coast of Buzen near Fukuoka. His opponent was Kojiro Sasaki, a young sword master who served as the kenjutsu instructor for the lord of his province.

Sasaki had developed a technique known as the "swallowtail cut" for its resemblance to a swallow's tail in flight. The cut was famous for its swiftness and power and was considered nearly unstoppable. The ambitious Sasaki was seeking fame as the man who defeated the invincible Musashi, and his lord agreed to sponsor a challenge match.

The time for the match had been set at eight in the morning on the beach of Ganryu Island. The VIP spectators became anxious when the appointed time came and passed. Finally, a messenger was sent to fetch Musashi, who was still fast asleep. Of course the always-clever Musashi may have deliberately overslept in order to ruin Sasaki's composure. As Musashi was being rowed over to the island, he made no attempt to neaten his scruffy appearance, but instead he contented himself by carving a wooden sword out of an old boat oar.

When the boat neared the beach, Musashi leaped ashore, holding the wooden sword aloft in a guard position. The irritated Sasaki drew his katana and tossed away the sheath. Musashi saw that gesture and said, "You are lost, for you have no more use for your sheath." The swordsmen stalked each other along the tideline, staring intensely into each other's eyes. Sasaki made a swift swallowtail cut but Musashi countered with a single perfect blow to Sasaki's forehead. Sasaki fell dead. All that Sasaki's strike had done was to cut Musashi's headband in half, spilling his long hair down into his face. The fight over, Musashi simply bowed to the assembled dignitaries, climbed back into his boat, and departed.

According to Eiji Yoshikawa's classic novel *Musashi*, the swordsman experienced a spiritual awakening as the boat pulled away from the island. For the only time in his life Musashi shed a tear for a fallen enemy. He would never fight another duel. But he would teach kenjutsu, and because of his skill as a strategist, Musashi would return to military service several times, often under the banner of his former enemies, the Tokugawas.

Despite his ruthlessness as a fighter, Musashi also became known as a great artist in his later years. His paintings, sculpture, and callig-raphy are among the finest in Japanese history. He was also an accomplished man of letters, known for his poems (now lost) and his masterwork, *The Book of Five Rings*, a guide to strategy and swordsmanship that was completed less than a month before he died of natural causes in 1645. Today, because of his relentless quest for perfection, Musashi is remembered as a *kenshi*, or "sword saint." For despite the violence of his life, he had truly dedicated himself to a higher calling.

JACKIE CHAN
(1954–   )

Jackie Chan was born in one of the worst slums in Hong Kong. His parents were so desperately poor that they tried to sell him to the doctor who delivered him, and by the time Chan was seven, his parents could no longer afford to care for him at all. He would have to learn how to survive and make a better life for himself on his own.

He was sent to Master Yu Chan-Luan's Chinese Drama Academy to study Peking Opera, a traditional form of Chinese theater that incorporates singing, dancing, kung fu, acting and acrobatics. In exchange for his training and his room and board, young Chan would spend the next ten years of his life slaving for Master Yu.

Life at the academy was harsh. Every day Chan and his classmates woke up at five in the morning, when the sky was still dark. Then they spent the entire day and evening training. Chan's exercises included staying in handstands for hours at a time or singing at the top of his lungs until he was hoarse and ready to faint with thirst. If Chan talked back or performed poorly, he was beaten with a stick or forced to go without food. Finally, at midnight,

Chan and his fellow students were sent to their quarters to sleep. There they huddled ten to a bed for warmth, knowing that in a few short hours another terrible day would begin.

When Chan graduated at age seventeen, he had mastered Peking Opera, but he had received so little formal schooling he could barely read or write. Worse yet, every month another traditional Chinese theater closed down forever, forcing dozens of actors to compete for the same parts. As the new kid on the block, Chan was passed over in favor of more established actors. The only place for someone with Chan's skills to turn was the wild and woolly Hong Kong film industry.

While Hollywood had multimillion-dollar budgets and six-month shooting schedules for some films, most Hong Kong movies of the era could be shot in as little as two weeks, often without any kind of written script. In this rough-and-tumble business, Chan quickly made a name for himself as a hardworking stuntman who was willing to take on even the most dangerous stunts. After Bruce Lee's death, Hong Kong moviemakers searched desperately for new stars, and Chan was among those chosen to succeed the Little Dragon. Chan starred in a number of serious kung fu flicks but they all bombed. It seemed that Chan just didn't have the raw animal presence of Lee.

He soon realized that simply joining the legion of cheap Bruce Lee clones would not be enough for him. Chan wanted to stand out from the crowd. He decided to succeed by being himself and by doing things his own way and not the way Bruce Lee would do them. He says,

STATE OF THE ART

It's not clear whether Chan ever mastered any single martial arts style, but he possesses more sheer physical ability, determination, and versatility than any other martial arts performer alive. He has demonstrated extensive knowledge of long-range northern Chinese kung fu styles, close-range southern styles such as wing chun, and even kickboxing. In addition, he is skilled with traditional Chinese weapons, including spears and swords.

"When Bruce Lee kick high, I kick low. When Bruce Lee punch, he is the superhero. When I punch, it hurts [me]. I do the funny face."

Putting his new philosophy into motion, Chan almost singlehandedly created an entirely new kind of movie: the kung fu action comedy. Inspired by silent film legends such as Buster Keaton, Harold Lloyd, and Charlie Chaplin, Chan added delightful physical comedy to his films. *Drunken Master* (1978) and *Fearless Hyena* (1979) broke all Hong Kong box-office records, including the ones set by Bruce Lee's movies. Chan was on his way.

Early in his career Chan made several attempts to cross over into Hollywood films. He co-starred with Burt Reynolds in *Cannonball Run* and *Cannonball Run II* and starred in *The Big Brawl,* and *The Protector*. None of the films did well.

American filmmakers just didn't know what to do with Chan and wouldn't let him be himself. Stunt coordinators with only a few years of experience told him how to punch. Directors would cast him as Japanese characters instead of Chinese and then tell him to act more like Bruce Lee or Clint Eastwood. To top it all off, Chan had a guest shot on *The Today Show* but was told just to do some kung fu moves and not to speak because his English wasn't good enough. He soon realized that Hollywood wasn't ready for him. Chan returned to Hong Kong where he was king.

But ruling the Asian cinema wasn't good enough. Chan was unsatisfied with the story limitations of the typical kung fu film, so starting with *Project A* in 1983, he began creating and performing some of the funniest and scariest stunts ever seen on the silver screen. That film included some scenes that have to be seen to be believed, including an absolutely hysterical bicycle chase through the back alleys of old Hong Kong. *Project A* created a revolution in the Hong Kong film industry and soon everyone was trying to copy Chan, but they couldn't capture his combination of humor, grace, and sheer nuttiness.

Chan has continued to be an innovator over the years. Some of his most outrageous and death-defying stunts include a fight on a bed of live coals while his pants leg was on fire and hooking onto a speeding doubledecker bus with an umbrella handle so that he could surf along the asphalt behind it.

DID YOU KNOW?

Jackie Chan's movies are so dangerous to make that none of the stuntmen can get health or life insurance. Chan pays all of their medical bills.

Always trying to please his fans and surpass himself has taken an enormous toll on Chan over the years; he is partially deaf in one ear and has broken almost every major bone in his body, including an ankle and both wrists. To this day, he still has a hole in his skull from when he nearly killed himself during a routine fall from a tree while filming *Armor of God* (1986). Yet, Chan somehow keeps bouncing back for more.

Recently, Jackie Chan made his second attempt at cracking the U.S. market as the star of the widely distributed, multimillion-dollar film called *Rumble in the Bronx*. It was a hit. Jackie Chan is now a bona fide Hollywood star.

WONG FEI HUNG*

(1847–1924)

Photo courtesy of Shooting Star

Fighter, teacher, healer, and revolutionary, Wong Fei Hung is remembered as all of these things and more. He was a true hero for troubled times and a constant protector of the weak and defenseless.

Wong Fei Hung was the son of Wong Kay Ying, a highly respected physician and martial artist from the city of Canton in China's Kwantung (Guangdong) Province. Wong Kay Ying's mastery of the martial arts was such that he was one of the original members of a group of near-legendary heroes known as "the Ten Tigers of Kwantung," an honor his son would later share.

Even as a young boy, Wong Fei Hung was already assisting at his father's famous clinic, the Bao Chi Lum. Wong Fei Hung learned traditional Chinese medicine at his father's side, but even more importantly, he learned generosity and compassion. His father, Wong Kay Ying, never turned away a patient, regardless of how poor or wretched he or she might be. Won Fei Hung also became a Chinese

---

*Five-time wushu champion Jet Li (pictured above) played Wong Fei Hung in the 1991 Hong Kong release *Once Upon a Time in China*.

patriot because his father secretly treated revolutionaries who were struggling against the oppressive and corrupt rule of the Ch'ing Dynasty.

The Manchu emperors of the Ch'ing (Qing) Dynasty had come from the northern land of Manchuria and were considered foreign invaders by the southern Chinese, even though they had ruled China for more than two centuries. The Manchus were ruthless in stomping out any signs of resistance, and one of their targets was the southern Shaolin Temple in Fukien (Fugian), a center for martial arts training that attracted many revolutionaries.

The Manchus attacked and burned the temple in 1734, but the unintended result of the destruction was that martial arts actually spread throughout China. The few fighting monks who escaped the attack journeyed throughout the land, teaching their skills to those who were willing to take up the fight against the Manchus. From the teaching of these wandering monks many new martial arts styles were born, including *wing chun* (Bruce

STATE OF THE ART

Hung ga kung fu is among the most famous of the Chinese martial arts. Like many other Chinese systems, its roots are in the arts of the southern Shaolin Temple. Hung ga styles include animal movements, hand techniques, weapons training, and powerful stances.

Hung Ga is equally balanced between hard "external" movements and softer "internal" training. This aspect is most evident in the tiger-fork form created by Wong Fei Hung. The tiger half of the sequence of movements is powerful and aggressive, with little defense. In contrast, the crane half is calm, balanced, and very defensive, with an emphasis on counterattacks executed with whip-like power.

Lee's original style) and *hung ga kung fu* (the art that Wong Fei Hung would later make famous).

One day when Wong Fei Hung was still a little boy, he saw his father practicing hung ga kung fu. He was fascinated and asked his father to teach it to him. Wong Kay Ying refused because he did not think his son was mature enough and because he feared the boy would become an object of suspicion by Manchu agents. But his father's refusal didn't stop Wong Fei Hung. The determined lad sought out his father's teacher, Luk Ah Choi.

The elderly Luk Ah Choi was impressed by the boy's spirit and agreed to teach him the basics of hung ga. Luk Ah Choi then chided Wong Kay Ying for not helping perpetuate the system. Chastened, Wong Kay Ying took over his son's training.

Wong Fei Hung followed in his father's footsteps. By his early twenties he had made a name for himself as a dedicated physician and a martial arts prodigy. Then he undertook the formalization of hung ga, creating its famed tiger-crane form and adding fighting combinations now known as the "nine special fists." His kick was so swift that it was called "the shadowless kick," supposedly because it was invisible to the normal human eye. The truth is slightly less romantic, but it reveals his cleverness as a fighter. He would distract his opponent with a crane strike to the eyes before launching a lightning kick from beneath the folds of his long coat.

Wong Fei Hung was also skilled with a great number of weapons, especially the long wooden staff and the southern tiger fork, a trident-like weapon. His skill with a staff served him well when he defeated a thirty-man gang on the docks of Canton.

A fearless defender of the weak and less fortunate, Wong Fei Hung protected many of his fellow citizens both from criminal gangs and government forces, who were often indistinguishable.

Wong Fei Hung traveled constantly throughout China, seeking out new medical knowledge. One day he came upon a small town that was being terrorized by a bandit chieftain who had a huge and

DID YOU KNOW?

More than 200 films have been made about the exploits of Wong Fei Hung. Legendary Hong Kong actor and martial artist Kwan Tak Hing starred in more than 100 of them over a period of five decades. Other martial arts stars who have portrayed Wong Fei Hung include Jackie Chan and the incredibly agile Jet Li, star of *Once Upon a Time in China* and its sequels.

vicious mastiff dog. The bandit sent the dog after anyone who resisted him. Wong Fei Hung confronted the chieftain, who immediately set the man-sized dog on him. The mastiff's huge fangs snapped on thin air as Wong Fei Hung neatly sidestepped the dog's charge. Then with a simultaneous kick to the chest and backfist to the head, the young master killed the enormous beast and turned toward the bandit, who ran away.

Despite his many triumphs, Wong Fei Hung's life also had great tragedy. Taking after his father, Wong Fei Hung's eldest son, Hawn Sum, strove to protect the poor and the weak of Canton. He was gunned down in the 1890s while in hot pursuit of the notorious Dai Fin Yee drug gang. After this heartrending loss, Wong Fei Hung vowed never to teach any of his remaining nine sons kung fu, lest they become targets as well.

Wong Fei Hung was also unlucky in love. His first three

wives died young, and he resigned himself to living out his remaining days alone. But his luck changed in 1903 at an outdoor martial arts demonstration. As he was performing a particularly vigorous section of the southern tiger-fork form, his shoe flew off into the audience and hit a sixteen-year-old girl named Mok Gwai Lan. The enraged girl leapt upon the stage and began berating the middle-aged master. Wong Fei Hung apologized profusely, but she told him "You're a master, so you have no excuse. What if it had been your weapon that hit me in the head?"

Enchanted by the girl's fiery spirit, Wong Fei Hung sought out her relatives and asked for her hand in marriage. They were honored by a proposal from such an eminent gentleman and quickly accepted his offer.

In time, Mok Gwai Lan came to be the master's strong right hand, for she was a skilled martial artist in her own right, helping her husband's hung ga demonstrations and teaching all of the women's classes at his school. She even taught many of the men's classes, which was unheard of since women of the era rarely mastered kung fu; it was considered unfeminine.

Wong Fei Hung died peacefully in 1924, a happy and humble man to the end. He always insisted that he was not a true master, but only a "bean curd martial artist." He meant he was as soft and vulnerable as bean curd. Despite his disavowal of his skill, Wong Fei Hung is deservedly remembered as one of China's greatest heroes.

BRUCE LEE
(1940–1973)

In 1959 Bruce Lee stepped off a boat from Hong Kong and onto the docks of San Francisco. It wasn't the first time the future kung fu superstar came to America. His father was a famous Hong Kong actor, Lee Hoi Chuen. On a tour of Chinese theaters in the United States, Mr. Lee and his wife, Grace, stopped in San Francisco where Grace Lee gave birth to Bruce. The family left San Francisco shortly after Bruce was born, and he didn't return until he was nearly twenty years old. But Bruce Lee was a natural-born American citizen.

As a youth in Hong Kong, Lee was a good student and a well-known child actor who appeared in numerous films. That was the good side. On the bad side, he liked to fight. He got into many street brawls, especially after he began learning wing chun kung fu from the great Master Yip Man.

Always ambitious, Lee decided to journey back to the United States to further his education. When he arrived, all that he had to his name was $100, five years of wing chun kung fu training, and the title of Hong Kong Cha-Cha Dance Champion of 1958.

STATE OF THE ART

Bruce Lee originally trained in wing chun kung fu, a southern Chinese system that specializes in close-range fighting. He then expanded wing chun with movements from other arts, especially the footwork and hand techniques of fencing and boxing.

Lee was concerned that most martial arts systems were too rigid. He encouraged his advanced students to cross-train in different systems and to absorb what was useful into their own personal style. Lee called his approach *jeet kune do*, and he always insisted that it was not a style but a way of thinking.

Settling in Seattle, Washington, Lee worked as a dishwasher at a Chinese restaurant while studying philosophy at the University of Washington. He also opened his first kung fu school.

After finishing school, Lee married Linda Emery and the couple moved to Oakland, California, where he opened the second of his schools. That didn't go over well with the local Chinese martial artists who felt that Lee should not be teaching non-Chinese students. Their anger led them to send kung fu teacher Won Jak Man to challenge Lee. If Lee prevailed he could continue teaching to the general public, but if he failed he would be forced to close his school. It was no contest. Lee hammered Won Jak Man into the ground.

But fighting Won Jak Man in the traditional wing chun style exhausted Lee. As he recovered from the fight, he felt he'd had a hard time landing clean shots on his opponent and that wing chun was limited and inefficient. The Won Jak Man fight prompted Lee to investigate new training and fighting methods, seeking to become a more versatile martial artist. He decided traditional kung fu was overly complicated and had drifted away from the essence of combat. Lee sought to create a more instinctive and effective martial art, one he eventually came to call *jeet kune do* (way of the intercepting fist).

One of Lee's greatest triumphs occurred at Ed Parker's Long Beach International Karate Championships in 1964. For a complete unknown like Bruce Lee to be invited to the tournament to show his talents was a great honor. Lee rose to the occasion and gave a spectacular demonstration of his skills, including his piledriver-like "one-inch punch."

That tournament was the beginning of the legend of Bruce Lee. It brought him to the attention of Hollywood producers, and he soon landed a role as Kato on *The Green Hornet* TV series. Lee became so popular in Asia that *The Green Hornet* was known as *The Kato Show*.

While working on *The Green Hornet*, Lee continued full blast with his martial arts training and teaching. His students included such famous people as full-contact karate champ Joe Lewis, Hall of Fame NBA center Kareem Abdul-Jabbar, and actors Steve McQueen and James Coburn—just to name a few.

Aside from fulfilling his personal ambition, Lee saw his Hollywood success as a chance to prove that Asian actors could be heroes and not just side-kicks or sinister villains. He came up with the concept for the *Kung Fu* TV series and was set to star in it when the part was given to David Carradine. It seemed that Hollywood executives weren't ready to accept the idea of an Asian leading man. Disgusted, Lee moved back to Hong Kong.

Lee left Hollywood, but he didn't leave the movies. In Hong Kong, he made three films for Raymond Chow's Golden Harvest Studios, breaking all Asian box-office records. That made Hollywood take notice. The American studio executives soon came calling, and Bruce Lee became an American star. Hollywood money made it possible for Lee to produce his masterpiece, *Enter the Dragon* in 1973. Tragically, he died just days before it premiered, apparently from an allergic reaction to a common headache pill.

Despite his premature death, Lee remains the single largest influence on the world of martial arts. His top student, Daniel Inosanto, still teaches the concepts of jeet kune do, and several of Lee's other students, such as Taky Kimura, Jesse Glover, and Ted Wong, continue to share their own individual interpretations of Lee's martial arts legacy. These and many other martial artists live by Lee's famous motto, "Absorb what is useful; reject what is useless."

JIGORO KANO

(1860–1938)

If any one man can be credited with modernizing the martial arts, it is Dr. Jigoro Kano, founder of Kodokan judo. Kodokan judo was the first Asian martial art based entirely on scientific principles of force and motion, rather than brute strength or mystic philosophy. As Kano himself put it, judo relies on "maximum efficiency with minimum effort."

Kano stressed that judo was not just about competition and self-defense. According to Kano the true *judoka* (judo practitioner) improves his or her mind and body for the benefit of society at large as much as for personal reasons. To set his students apart from others, Kano introduced the pajama-like *gi* as a uniform for judo artists. The gi was both a practical garment and a symbolic one. It was heavy enough so that it wouldn't tear when it was grabbed during a match, and its single-color design—usually white or black—resembled the garments of some Buddhist monks. To allow students to display their level of expertise in his new martial art, Kano devised a system of colored belts ranking from white to red to be worn with the gi.

How did one man come to give so much to the martial arts?

Kano was born near Kobe, Japan, just as the 264-year reign of the Tokugawa Shoguns (military rulers) came to an end. The Tokugawa Shoguns were a family of generals who ruled Japan in the name of the emperor from 1603 to 1867. Their power stemmed from the military and diplomatic skills of Ieyasu Tokugawa, who united Japan under his rule after a great battle at Sekigahara in 1600. The Tokugawa rulers feared the influence of Western culture and were afraid that one of their rivals would team with a European power and overthrow them. As such they banned most contact with Western trade missions or military forces. They were overthrown in a short and relatively bloodless civil war called the Meiji Revolution.

By the time the Emperor Meiji reclaimed imperial power from the shoguns in 1868, Japan had become an isolated backwater nation, struggling to join the modern world. The emperor called for his people to build a new nation to match the great world powers of the time, including the United States and Great Britain.

Into this whirlwind of change stepped Jigoro Kano, the son of a wealthy and respectable man who supported

STATE OF THE ART

On its surface, judo appears to be little more than a form of jacketed wrestling that emphasizes throws, locks, and ground fighting. But Kano also emphasized self-defense, competition, and physical exercise. The most important concept in the art is *ju*, which can be loosely translated as "flexibility." A good judo practitioner can adapt to any situation, both in the dojo and in everyday life.

Japan's rapid modernization. Kano's father urged him to study English and higher mathematics, as well as traditional subjects such as Chinese and Japanese literature and calligraphy. In Kano's youth, Japan did not have enough textbooks to go around; students often had to read them in shifts. So Kano was only able to study

English from 1 A.M. to 5 A.M. Nevertheless, Kano gained such mastery of English that he used the language to write his journal and judo technical notes. Kano respected tradition, but he was a forward thinker who believed in the new spirit of the era.

Historically, times of enormous change present great dangers as well as great opportunities, and Japan's Meiji Revolution was no exception. With the Shogun's harsh government in shambles, the law had almost completely broken down. Bands of hardened criminals roamed freely throughout the country, robbing and beating anyone they wished to. Against the backdrop of this lawlessness, Kano decided that it would be good to know how to protect himself, so he began to study the martial arts. He did so despite warnings from his father and others that the Japanese martial arts were old-fashioned and useless.

Kano learned many arts, including boxing and wrestling, but he concentrated on traditional Japanese jujutsu. When he was seventeen he began studying the *tenshin shin'yo ryu* style of jujutsu, which is known for its strikes on *atemi* (vital points) and its grappling techniques. A few years later, Kano also began training in the *kito-ryu* style, which focuses on techniques for throwing one's opponent to the ground.

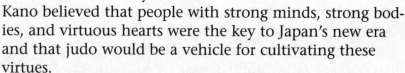

Kano's belief in progress led him to open his own training hall, which he called the *Kodokan*, or "the Institute for the Study of the Way." At the ripe age of twenty-two, he already had a grand vision for the role of the martial arts in Japan's future. The new art he was developing would be called *judo* (the "gentle" or "flexible" way) and wouldn't just be a combat art but a way of life. Kano believed that people with strong minds, strong bodies, and virtuous hearts were the key to Japan's new era and that judo would be a vehicle for cultivating these virtues.

Kano was disturbed by the fact that many jujutsu men of the era were common street brawlers or even gang enforcers, so his new art emphasized exercise and safe competition as much as fighting.

Less than twenty years after Kano refined jujutsu into judo, it had become one of the most popular martial arts in Japan. Judo was embraced by Japanese looking for something modern that was also from their own culture. During the late 1880s Kano was sent on several tours around the world by the Japanese government. His mission was to study foreign cultures and educational methods. The tours also gave Kano a chance to show the rest of the world a little Japanese culture.

He later dispatched a number of senior students on overseas judo demonstration tours. U.S. President Theodore Roosevelt was among the world leaders who were truly impressed by the "gentle way." Roosevelt even took up judo himself, reaching brown-belt level.

DID YOU KNOW?

In the entire history of the Kodokan only thirteen men have ever earned their tenth dan (degree) or red belt. The ranking system actually goes all the way to twelfth dan, but no one, not even Dr. Kano, has ever achieved that rank.

By the turn of the century, Kano was one of the most respected men in Japan. He even served as an advisor to many top figures in the Japanese government. In fact he was so well known around the world that he became the unofficial Japanese Ambassador-at-Large, and in 1909 he was appointed Japan's representative on the International Olympic Committee (IOC).

Kano held the IOC post for nearly twenty years. His greatest achievement in that job came at the IOC conference in Cairo, Egypt, in 1938 when he arranged for the 1940 Summer Olympics to be held in Tokyo. Unfortunately, the 1940 Olympics were never held because of the outbreak of World War II. Kano would have been horrified by the war's death and destruction, for he always believed in building bridges between different peoples and nations. He never was to know about the catastrophe that would strike Japan and the rest of the world; he died on the sea voyage home from Cairo at the age of seventy-eight. Today Kano's dream lives on at the Kodokan, where every year tens of thousands of students from all over the world are trained in judo.

GICHIN FUNAKOSHI
(1868–1957)

G ichin Funakoshi,
the man who
introduced karate to Japan, was a native
of Okinawa, a small island in the East China Sea.
Okinawa is a harsh and beautiful place, with barely
enough farmland to support the population. Turning to
the fickle sea for their survival through trade and fishing,
the Okinawans became a hardy and self-sufficient people.

For centuries the people of Okinawa lived in an independent kingdom. But the island kingdom was too close
to Japan and not strong enough to fight off the Japanese.
By the 1600s the Japanese controlled Okinawa, both
politically and militarily. Today the island is a prefecture
(state) of Japan.

Even after Okinawa was conquered by the Japanese in
1609, the islanders strove to retain a spirit of indepen-
dence. Training in karate and its companion art, *kobujutsu*,
was banned and it had to take place in secret, often at
night, deep in the forest, or on a secluded beach. Because
of this secrecy, there are significant differences between
each of the karate styles practiced on Okinawa today, even
though the island is only forty-five miles long.

Because Okinawa is on a major trade route, the islanders were exposed to the fighting arts of many Asian nations over the last thousand years, particularly those of China and Japan. Over time, native Okinawan arts blended with foreign styles to become the art of *te* (hand). Te was later called *karate* (China hand) to honor the strong influence of the Chinese arts.

Gichin Funakoshi was born into a family of classical scholars. A premature baby, he was not expected to live. But he survived and grew into a remarkably healthy boy, although he was always tiny for his age. Bright and disciplined, Funakoshi followed family tradition by becoming a keen student of classic Chinese literature, reading the works of Confucius, Lao Tzu, and other philosophers.

As Funakoshi grew to manhood, a wave of modernization and reforms swept through Japan and onto Okinawa. On the one hand stood zealous reformers who wanted to bring Okinawa into a new era. On the other side stood the ancient families of the island who wanted to preserve tradition and feared the loss of status the coming changes would bring. Funakoshi was trapped between the two parties and even lost a scholarship to the prestigious Tokyo Medical College because his family refused to allow him to attend a school that would make him shave off his topknot, a traditional sign of rank among Okinawan nobility.

Funakoshi was respectful of tradition, but he knew his destiny lay in the modern world. In 1888 he shaved off his topknot and accepted a teaching position in the Okinawan capitol of Naha, much to the dismay of his parents.

In Naha, Funakoshi married and eventually fathered

three sons and a daughter. His wife was a strong woman who was known for her piety and her skill at resolving neighborhood disputes. In spite of her many household responsibilities, she also found time to study karate alongside her husband, even leading classes in his absence.

It was in this period that Funakoshi truly attempted to master karate, studying primarily under Master Azato and Master "Ankoh" Itosu, the first man to teach karate publicly. Funakoshi trained relentlessly under the two instructors, learning basics and studying *kata* (or prearranged sequences of techniques). Under Itosu, Funakshi spent ten years perfecting just three basic kata.

Even when not directly supervised by his teachers, the gifted Okinawan continued honing his skills. He toughened his limbs by constantly striking the *makiwara*, a rope-covered wooden post. During typhoons, he even climbed up onto his roof and settled into a strong "horse stance" to face the raging storm.

Because of his obvious dedication, Funakoshi also had opportunities to train with many of the other great karate

STATE OF THE ART

Shotokan karate is a hard-punching and kicking style. Blocks tend to be direct rather than circular, and the footwork is very linear and aggressive. Shotokan experts are known for the power and precision of their strikes. In theory, they should be able to stop or disable an opponent with a single blow.

Shotokan also features extensive *kata*, or forms training. Kata are used to condition the body and train specific techniques. They are the heart of any traditional karate system because they contain all of the hidden practical applications of the art.

masters of the era, including Sokon Matsumura, the chief martial arts instructor and bodyguard of many of the kings of Okinawa.

By the turn of the century, karate was slowly emerging from its veil of secrecy, and Funakoshi was instrumental in the art's public acceptance. He gave demonstrations and toured throughout the island with other masters. Japanese military officials noticed that many of their Okinawan recruits were in top physical condition and soon sent many of their officers to the island to study karate.

In 1917 Funakoshi was invited to give a demonstration in Kyoto, Japan. It was the first time that karate had been formally presented outside of Okinawa. The exhibition went well, but there was no immediate boom in popularity for karate.

Four years later Funakoshi gave a special demonstration for the Japanese Crown Prince Hirohito. As a result Funakoshi was asked to represent Okinawan karate at the First National Athletic Exhibition in Tokyo. A meticulous man, he carefully prepared his demonstration and accompanying lecture, knowing that he would be facing the cream of Japanese society.

The demonstration was a rousing success, and Funakoshi was asked by Dr. Jigoro Kano and other prominent figures to stay in Japan to teach karate. Recently retired and well into his middle years, Funakoshi faced the prospect of starting a new life with great fear. But he knew there might never again be such a golden opportunity for karate, and he decided to stay. Funakoshi's wife supported his decision, but she remained in Okinawa because of family and religious obligations.

Although Funakoshi was warmly welcomed at the Kodokan, where he taught for some time, life in Tokyo was quite difficult. Funakoshi was clearly a cultured gentleman, but most Japanese look down upon Okinawans as backward country cousins. The great teacher and karate master faced many instances of prejudice.

Scraping by on the edge of poverty, Funakoshi was forced to take a number of menial jobs while he wrote about karate and slowly built up a core group of dedicated students. His big break came when Japanese universities began establishing karate clubs, broadening his student base. He was joined in Tokyo by his third son, Gigo, an immensely talented *karateka* (karate practitioner) who served as Funakoshi's chief assistant instructor. And Funakoshi's growing popularity soon paved the way for other Okinawan masters to come to Japan to teach karate.

DID YOU KNOW?

Kobujutsu is a weapons art that is an integral companion to Okinawan karate. The weapons were mostly derived from common farming implements and included the long *bo* (staff), the *kama* (sickle), the *nunchaku* (rice flail), the *sai* (short pitchfork used to catch enemy weapons), and the *tonfa* (baton with a side handle used today by many American police officers). Oddly enough Funakoshi did not incorporate kobujutsu training into Shotokan karate, perhaps because he was emphasizing self-improvement and not mortal combat.

By 1936 Funakoshi was successful enough to open a large *dojo*, called the Shotokan, after his pen name, Shoto (pine waves). That year he also changed the Chinese character in the word karate from "China hand" to "empty hand," which signified many things besides unarmed combat, including emptiness of ego and selflessness. Like

Dr. Kano, Funakoshi viewed the martial arts not just as fighting but as an education for an ethical way of life.

At the Shotokan, philosophical differences soon sprang up between father and son. Gigo favored adding karate competitions to attract young and active students. His father felt that true karate was too dangerous to use in free-sparring. Regardless of their opinions, however, both enforced incredibly high standards, causing nine out of ten students to drop out within their first year.

Karate in Japan took on a dark aspect during World War II. Students trained feverishly, knowing that they might have to use their skills in a life-or-death situation. The end of the war proved to be tragic for Funakoshi. The Shotokan and much of Tokyo was burned to the ground by American bombing raids, and his son, Gigo, died of leukemia.

Worse, Okinawa had been devastated in battle, with more than 60,000 civilian deaths. Ninety percent of the survivors were left homeless and starving. Somehow Funakoshi's wife managed to escape the island and rejoin her husband in Japan, where she became ill. He was unable to afford adequate food and proper medical care for her during her illness, and she died of asthma two years later.

Despite his grief, Funakoshi worked diligently to rebuild karate, forming the Japan Karate Association in 1949. The organization was established to set rigorous technical and ethical standards for karate, but many of the post-war generation of karateka were more interested in competition than learning the fundamentals of their art.

Still, Funakoshi was able to build a talented corps of instructors whom he dispatched around the world to spread his true Shotokan karate. Today Shotokan is the single most popular karate style in the world. When Funakoshi died of natural causes at eighty-nine, he could rightfully say that he had done more for karate than any other man.

RENA "RUSTY" KANOKOGI

(1935–)

Photo courtesy of C. H. Halporm

Rena Glickman was born during the height of the Great Depression on Coney Island, New York, home of some of America's greatest amusement parks. Hard times bred strong-minded people, and by age five Rena and a friend named Renee decided their names sounded too "soft." They chose to call themselves "Rusty" and "Rex" in honor of some extremely large neighborhood dogs. Rusty's nickname stuck because of her red hair.

In the carnival atmosphere of World War II-era Coney Island, Rusty saw a chance to be a "street entrepreneur." One of her most profitable "businesses" was selling ice water to thirsty tourists. Always looking for an angle, she decided to sell confetti to partiers in local bars, figuring that drunks made better tippers. She even got a dollar tip from Lon Chaney, Jr., moviedom's original Wolf Man.

In her free time, Rusty hung around performers from Coney Island's famous sideshows, including the strong men, sword swallowers, and bearded ladies. "It was every-

35

one from the good, the bad, and the ugly," she recalls.

Rusty was always a strong and athletic girl, but because there were few organized sports for women, she had no outlets for her energy. All she could do was go to the local gym, where she learned how to punch the heavy bag. In fact, she punched so hard that not only did she move the bag, she moved the man holding it. She also began weightlifting, although her weights were a bit unusual: Lacking traditional dumbbells, she used the heavy weighted bus-stop signs that were found on the street corners.

A tough, feisty kid, Rusty never backed down from a fight. As a teenager, her combativeness helped her become leader of an all-girl street gang called the Apaches.

During her gang years, Rusty was definitely a "youth at risk." Fortunately, when she was nineteen, a family friend introduced her to judo. She said to herself, "That's for

STATE OF THE ART

In her personal approach to judo, Rusty Kanokogi emphasizes the importance for each student to develop his or her own style, since different techniques work better for different body types. But regardless of the size of the student, she tells them to "always bother their opponent's feet and always take their feet away with foot sweeps. Once you take away the foundation, any house will fall, no matter how big and strong it is." Rusty herself likes to rely on the *harai-goshi* (reaping loin) hip throw, which requires perfect blending of timing, power, and balance; it is considered one of the centerpieces of judo technique.

Today Rusty teaches judo to hundreds of students every week. She teaches at public schools, private schools, alternative schools for kids at risk, colleges and at her own Kyushu Dojo, which she founded with her husband, Ryohei.

me," when she saw that it involved "throwing people to the ground, hard." She began training at the YMCA under Master Saiganji, a stern instructor from Japan who liked to recount long World War II stories as his students sat in *seiza*, or kneeling practice. He would ramble on as their legs knotted up with cramps.

There were only a few other female judo students at the time, and they mostly concentrated on *kata* (forms practice), which didn't particularly interest Rusty. She was drawn to *randori* (fighting practice). Soon she started training full time with the men in her class. A few of them might have been put off by having to fight a woman, but most came to respect the fact that Rusty could take anything they could dish out and serve it right back to them.

For the next eight years Rusty trained like a madwoman, taking on anyone who would go to the mat with her and entering every local judo competition. She recalls the joy she felt when she received her brown belt. "That was my happiest rank," she says. "I could control all of the colored belts [below brown]." She adds that it felt great to defeat a black belt because she was the underdog.

In 1962, the time had finally come for Rusty to test for her black belt. Before an examining board of high-ranking Japanese black belts, Rusty was matched with other female students from different schools in the New York area. They were told to demonstrate their skills but to more or less "take it easy on each other." About halfway through the test, Saiganji gave Rusty a look that meant "be aggressive"—and Rusty not only earned her first-degree black belt but was also offered an opportunity to train at the Kodokan (the Institute for the Study of the Way), judo's central institute in Tokyo, Japan.

Rusty spent nearly a year at the Kodokan, learning as much as possible about judo. She knew she would have to earn the respect of the other *judoka* (judo students) at the Kodokan, so she practiced so hard that the Japanese began calling her "judo crazy."

Being judo crazy paid off. Rusty showed so much focus and willingness to learn that she became the first woman ever invited to train at "the Mecca of judo," the Kodokan's main *dojo* (training hall)—previously she had been restricted to the smaller and less-intense women's and foreigners' dojos. In the main dojo, Rusty trained seven days a week, starting at nine in the morning under Master Inokuma, whom she dubbed "the Beast from the East." After being put through the wringer every

morning, she spent the entire afternoon in a special class for high-ranking instructors. As Rusty now puts
it, "I only *thought* I knew judo
until I went to Japan."

When Rusty earned her second
dan, it was personally awarded to
her by Rissei Kano, the son of
Dr. Jigoro Kano, the founder
of judo.

After Rusty returned from
Japan, she concentrated on offici-
ating matches and teaching
judo full time in Brooklyn and
Manhattan. She also married
Ryohei Kanokogi, a good
friend and extraordinarily
skilled judoka whom she
met at the Kodokan and
who had since moved to
the United States. Rusty calls their relationship "a thirty-
one-and-a-half-year marriage of opposites." Ryohei
Kanokogi is a quiet and serene man who is the descen-
dant of an ancient samurai family from the southern
Japanese island of Kyushu. Rusty is a self-described "madwoman" from Coney Island in the south of Brooklyn.
Together they are perhaps the most respected pair of judo
instructors in the United States today.

Remembering her own limited opportunities, Rusty
Kanokogi has tried to create more opportunities in competitive sports for girls and women. Her most well-known
struggle was to get women's judo designated an official
Olympic event. The main obstacle was the rigidly bureau-
cratic International Olympic Committee. It took nearly
twenty years, but in the end the IOC caved in, largely
because of Rusty's efforts. Women's judo became a
demonstration sport for the 1988 Olympics in Seoul,
South Korea, and was admitted as a medal sport in the

1992 Olympics in Barcelona, Spain. As the icing on the cake, Rusty was named coach of the 1988 U.S. women's judo team.

Today Rusty Kanokogi is a fifth-degree black belt and in line for her sixth *dan*. That makes her the highest-ranking woman judoka in North America. She also continues to serve in countless organi-

zations on the local and national level to promote active participation in sports, especially for women and "kids at risk." As one of her students put it, "no matter how wound up you get, judo always puts you back on track." Rusty says her only regret is that she never personally got to compete in the Olympics and bring back a gold medal for the United States. She says some of the best things about judo are being a part of a worldwide family and "never feeling alone." She advises, "you're never finished learning."

JHOON RHEE

(1932–   )

Grandmaster Jhoon Rhee's early days held few hints that he would one day become one of the world's most prominent martial artists. Only eleven months after his birth in Asan, Korea, his older sister accidentally dropped him on the ground, shattering his thigh. The very same day his maternal grandfather died. Rhee's mother bundled up her infant son and carried him five miles to her father's deathbed. Following a popular folk belief, she used her departed father's hand to massage the baby's broken leg. Amazingly, the fractured bone healed quickly and cleanly, with only one visit to the doctor.

When Rhee was five, he was sent to live with his uncle and paternal grandfather, and his cousins were sent to his parents' home. The theory was that a child could not always have his way with his uncles and aunts as he might with his own parents. By living apart from his parents, Rhee was expected to become more self-reliant. His grandfather was a stern but loving man who taught his grandson the importance of honesty, discipline, respect for one's elders, and a love of learning, values that Master Rhee cherishes to this day.

After a year with his relatives, Rhee returned home. Puny for his age, he was frequently picked on by other children. One day when he was six, Rhee came home crying that a five-year-old neighborhood girl had slapped him. The words were hardly out of his mouth when his mother slapped him again. She was angry that he had allowed himself to be hit.

As Rhee grew into a teenager he was sent away to high school in Seoul, where he continued to be bullied by other kids. It was hardly unusual for him to return from school bruised and bloodied. Humiliated, Rhee vowed to find a way to defend himself. When he was thirteen, he found his opportunity and enrolled in the Chung Do Kwan, an early *tae kwon do* school.

The training soon paid off. One day in eleventh grade, the meanest and toughest of Rhee's tormentors took a pencil right out of his hand during class and refused to return it. Unable to take any more abuse, Rhee challenged the other kid to a fight after school. When the time came, Rhee must have felt like he was walking to his execution in the schoolyard, but it was too late to back out. As soon as they came face to face, his nemesis took a big swing at Rhee's head. Rhee ducked, fired off a punch to his opponent's left eye, and snapped out a side kick that took all the fight out of him in an instant. In a few short seconds, Rhee earned the respect of the entire school and threw off his schoolyard oppressors forever. "I personally gained peace through strength," he says.

DID YOU KNOW?

At sixty-four, the five-foot, six-inch Rhee can still jump kick nearly seven feet in the air and do 100 push-ups per minute. He has publicly vowed that he is going to live to be at least 137 years old, making him the oldest person ever. At that time he intends to do one push-up for each year of his age without resting.

Two years later, in 1950, Rhee was set to attend college but the Korean War broke out. Hordes of Communist troops poured down from North Korea, driving everyone before them. Eighteen-year-old Rhee and his nine-year-old brother, Jun, fled south to his grandfather's house. After a month the two boys became worried for their parents and decided to return home to their village to look for them. The journey home was truly perilous, for all of the roads were being shelled and bombed by U.S. forces intent on stopping the North Korean invasion.

Kindhearted villagers provided shelter for the two brothers each night after their grueling day's hike. Rhee and his brother finally reached their home after three

days of dodging airstrikes, but their hearts sank when
their mother was nowhere to be found. They feared she
was dead, but an hour later she came home. She had
merely been scrounging up extra food to supplement the
family's meager provisions. The reunion was a joyous one,
but now they were all trapped by advancing Communist
forces. Rhee was forced to hide in his cellar for two
months to avoid being forcibly drafted into the North
Korean Army.

Their village was liberated by American troops that winter, and Rhee, an excellent English student, gratefully
went to work as an interpreter. He would not see his family again for nearly four years.

The war was still raging, and Rhee was eventually drafted
into the South Korean Army, where he and his fellow sol-
diers were brutally treated by their superiors. They were
only allowed to sleep three or four hours a night, and their
daily rations consisted of three spoons of rice and a couple
of sips of salt-water "soup." The unit actually had better

STATE OF THE ART

Tae kwon do (the way of kicking and punching) is descended
from tae kyon, an ancient Korean art banned by the Japanese
when they invaded and occupied Korea from 1910 to 1945. The
art is famous for its spectacular kicks, including the spinning back
kick, flying side kick, hook kick, crescent kick, and downward
chopping axe kick. Practitioners of tae kwon do also learn to
break anything from wooden boards, bricks, and ceramic tiles to
slabs of stone and blocks of ice.

Jhoon Rhee's particular brand of tae kwon do uses a more
upright and mobile stance than is traditional, with more evasive
footwork.

food, but their corrupt commanding officer had sold most of their supplies on the black market, enriching himself on the misery of his men.

Things got so bad that Rhee jumped at the chance to go to officer's candidate school, even though he knew that seventy percent of all new officers were killed in battle. Although he enjoyed the temporary respite from his miserable unit, in the back of Rhee's mind there always lurked the fact that he had less than a one-in-three chance of surviving his new rank.

Luck shined on Rhee. Just two weeks before his graduation the war ended. Rhee's death sentence was commuted by the truce that was signed on June 27, 1953.

Rhee stayed in the army and managed to get himself sent to the United States in 1956 for additional training. He was stationed for six months in San Marcos, Texas, and quickly grew to love the people there for their honesty and hospitality. Rhee knew that when his assignment was over he wanted to find a way to return to the United States permanently. He found a sponsor and returned to Texas following his honorable discharge from the South Korean Army.

Rhee studied engineering at San Marcos State College and the University of Texas. To help finance his education, he began teaching tae kwon do. It was the first time that the Korean art had ever been seen in North America. It was also the start of a business empire that now includes more than forty schools nationwide and nearly seventy affiliated schools in the former Soviet Union.

Within two years Rhee achieved national prominence and was invited to attend Ed Parker's Long Beach Internationals in 1964. There Rhee met a young Bruce Lee. The two became fast friends and began training together whenever the opportunity arose. Rhee introduced Lee to all the long-range kicks of tae kwon do, including the powerful side kick that was to become one of Bruce's trademarks. In turn, Lee showed Rhee less traditional and more mobile footwork and stances, as well as

quicker and more precise hand techniques. Rhee remembers those days
fondly, recalling that whenever
Bruce came over, "My wife fixed
him a huge plate of sushi, and
we would eat and train like
mad until four or five in the
morning."

In addition to his modifi-
cations to traditional tae kwon
do, Jhoon Rhee has made many
other significant contributions
to the martial arts. He invented
the first line of foam rubber pro-
tective sparring gear, and he has
trained such notable champions
and teachers as Allen Steen and
Jeff Smith. His students have
also included Secret Service
agents, Pentagon personnel, and many Senators and
U.S. Representatives. In 1975, he even staged the
Congressional Grudge Match, where leading Republicans
and Democrats duked it out.

These days, Rhee fills in his already hectic schedule by
promoting fitness for senior citizens, giving motivational
speeches, and conducting frequent martial arts seminars.
Recalling his own difficult childhood, he helps with
young people through his "Joy of Discipline" program
featured at many Washington-area schools. The program
promotes knowledge, physical fitness, and self-esteem and
requires that all of the students maintain at least a B grade
average before being allowed to test for their black belts.
Rhee has not only lived the American dream, he is helping to bring it to others.

MORIHEI UESHIBA

(1883–1969)

Morihei Ueshiba, the founder of the Japanese art of *aikido* (the way of harmony), was in many ways a man not of his own time. He was a throwback to an older, more primal age. Unlike his contemporaries, Dr. Jigoro Kano and Gichin Funakoshi, who took a scientific approach to their discipline, Ueshiba relied on a more intuitive, almost mystical approach to the martial arts.

The mystical side of Ueshiba's character was strongly stamped by his birthplace, Tanabe village, in Wakayama Prefecture. His home was on the Pacific Ocean at the base of the sacred Kumano Mountains. For centuries, the Kumano range was known as a place of spiritual power, attracting holy men, mystics, and mad hermits, as well as devout pilgrims from Japan's two major religions, Shinto and Buddhism.

Ueshiba was born into a family of prominent landowners. His father was a well-respected man who served as a village official for more than two decades. His mother was a very religious woman who made daily pilgrimages to pray at local shrines. By the time Ueshiba was five, he was rising at 4 A.M. to make the rounds with her. On their way, she would fill her son's head with tales of divinely inspired men and powerful spirits of the region. Even as a young boy he began to believe that he was destined for great things.

A dreamer by nature, Ueshiba was fascinated by the stories of gods, demons, and heroes that he read about in the ancient Chinese classics. This worried his father who feared that his son might turn into a bookish and sickly young man. So he had the boy spend as much time as possible outdoors. Every day young Ueshiba would tramp through the mountains and fields or swim in the ocean. It was in these golden days that he developed his deep and abiding respect and connection with nature.

By 1902 Ueshiba was a young man bursting with energy but with no defined mission in life. He set off to the bustling metropolis of Tokyo where he opened a small but profitable stationery business and spent his evenings studying the many martial arts that were being taught in the city, including *jujutsu* and *kenjutsu*. His relentless schedule soon took a toll on him, and in less than a year he had fallen sick and was forced to return home to Tanabe to recuperate.

As he was being nursed back to health, Ueshiba fell in love with a young girl named Hatsu Itogawa, and they were soon married. The couple would eventually have three sons; only the youngest, Kisshomaru, survived into adulthood. When Ueshiba was well enough to leave the house, he took to hiking in the hills, swinging a heavy sword for exercise.

Knowing that war was imminent between Japan and

Russia, Ueshiba trained himself to peak physical condition, for he hoped to join the army and become a hero and a leader of men. His wish came true. Ueshiba was drafted into the Imperial Japanese Army where he became known as the "Man of Iron" because of his strength and incredible physique. Despite his short stature (five feet, two inches) and small frame, he weighed in at an incredible 180 pounds.

During his tour of duty, Ueshiba also continued his study of the martial arts, earning his first jujutsu teaching license and becoming truly fearsome with the sword, spear, and bayonet. He served with distinction during the Russo-Japanese War (1904–05), but it remains unclear if he ever saw any hand-to-hand combat. Because of his distinguished service, Ueshiba was selected for officer training, but his father didn't want his only son becoming a career military man and persuaded him to return to Tanabe.

Ueshiba returned home, but he still didn't have a sense of his destiny. Frustrated, he began acting erratic, locking himself in his room for hours at a time in prayer or vanishing into the wild for days on end. Everyone began to

STATE OF THE ART

Aikido is an art that stresses throws and locks. An aikido expert never matches brute strength with equal force. Instead, he uses his opponent's force to his own advantage.

In the last twenty-five years, aikido was practiced by many students as a kind of moving meditation rather than a combat art. But action star Steven Seagal has revived interest in the older, more aggressive form of aikido that Ueshiba favored before World War II.

wonder if Ueshiba was cracking up until his father built a small *dojo*, or training hall, on the family's property. Ueshiba trained like a maniac, finally able to vent some of his nervous energy.

In 1910 Ueshiba got a chance to put his energies to good use when he was asked to lead a group of eighty-four pioneers from overcrowded southern Japan to form a settlement on the northernmost island of Hokkaido. He proved to be a resolute and effective leader, bringing the colony to self-sufficiency and prosperity even in the face of blizzards, poor crop yields, and a massive fire that destroyed much of the settlers' property. On several occasions Ueshiba even had to use his martial arts skills to defend the tiny village from wild animal attacks and bandit raids.

He had been living in Hokkaido for five years when he first met Sokaku Takeda (1860–1943), the Grandmaster of the ancient *daito-ryu aikiju-jutsu* system, an art that included both extensive weapons and unarmed training. Takeda wandered throughout Japan, honing his skill in challenge matches in dojos and in life-or-death fights with vicious criminals. He rarely stayed in any area for more than a few months at a time, so few of his students ever mastered the daito-ryu system.

Ueshiba was astounded by the ease with which the tiny Takeda tossed around men more than twice his size during a public demonstration of his art. He bowed down before the master and asked to become his disciple. Takeda accepted him as his private student. In return, the normally strong-willed Ueshiba waited on the master hand and foot, seeing to his every need. Despite his heavy responsibilities as the head of the settlement, Ueshiba found time to master the very subtle techniques and principles of the enormously complex daito-ryu system, eventually earning another teaching license.

DID YOU KNOW?

The daito-ryu system of aikido contained several thousand individual techniques, yet Ueshiba was so skilled that he is said to have earned his teaching license in only one year of concentrated study.

Ueshiba's sojourn in Hokkaido ended in 1919 when he was called home to Tanabe to be by the side of his dying father. The journey was long and arduous, and by the time Ueshiba arrived in Tanabe, his father was already dead, leaving behind only a few words of encouragement for his son, "Do not be constrained; live the way you really want."

Grief-stricken, Ueshiba sought comfort in religion, joining the controversial *Omoto-kyo* sect, an offshoot of Shinto. The sect was headed by Onisaburo Deguchi, a charismatic man who preached that even everyday actions should be treated as art and made sacred. To that end Deguchi encouraged Ueshiba to refine and develop his knowledge of the fighting arts so that he could someday present the true essence of the martial arts to the entire world.

Ueshiba soon became the sect's chief martial arts

instructor as well as Deguchi's personal bodyguard. In 1924 Deguchi and Ueshiba embarked on their disastrous "great Mongolian adventure," which began when Deguchi decided to establish an ideal religious community on the remote steppes of Mongolia.

Deguchi's party hooked up with a bandit chief named Lu, whose troops served as an escort on the long journey across China to Mongolia. Local warlords, other bandits, and the Chinese army regarded the party as interlopers and reacted violently. The group came under heavy fire on numerous occasions, and Ueshiba was often obliged to draw his sword and engage in deadly combat to defend Deguchi. In the end, the entire party was captured by the Chinese army. Lu and his 130 men were executed without any trial, but there was a last minute reprieve for Ueshiba and the other Japanese members of the expedition, who were later deported back to Japan.

Ueshiba had exhibited uncanny skill while in Mongolia, seeming always to be aware of impending ambushes and able to sidestep attackers with ease. When he returned to Japan, he intensified his training at his dojo, to the point where many students simply couldn't keep up with him. He was able to throw multiple opponents high in the air in a matter of seconds and paralyze attackers with a single powerful *kiai* (shout).

As word spread of Ueshiba's prowess, many high-ranking military officers, wealthy businessmen, and aristocrats began traveling to the Omoto-kyo compound in Ayabe (near Kyoto) to train with him.

In 1926 Ueshiba moved to Tokyo and opened a dojo that soon became the training hall of Japan's elite. Despite aikido's current reputation for gentleness, training in Ueshiba's school was anything but soft, and broken bones were a regular occurrence. In 1933 Dr. Jigoro Kano, the founder of judo, visited Ueshiba's dojo and was so astounded by Ueshiba's skill that he said, "This is my ideal *budo* (martial art); it is true and genuine judo." Kano immediately dispatched many of his top judo men to study with Ueshiba.

When World War II broke out in 1941, Ueshiba continued training military officers, many of whom were assigned to secret units. Ueshiba quickly grew disenchanted with the war and about training Japan's elite forces. He was appalled by the carnage in World War II. Realizing nothing he taught could help his students defend themselves against heavy artillery, machine guns, or aerial bombs, Ueshiba closed his dojo and retired to his farm in the countryside.

After the war Ueshiba adopted a new approach to martial arts training. Aikido training became a spiritual endeavor, designed to bring the practitioner into harmony with himself and the universe. He stressed complete adaptability, saying, "Depending on the circumstance, your movements should be as hard as a diamond, flexible as a willow, smooth-flowing like water, or as empty as space."

Ueshiba's new message of peace, harmony, and balance found a receptive audience in an atomic age dominated by the possibility of total world destruction. In the two decades following the war, aikido spread far and wide, and today millions of aikido practitioners strive to live by and promote Ueshiba's teaching.

CHUCK NORRIS

(1940–   )

Chuck Norris was born in Oklahoma at the end of the Great Depression. In his biography, *The Secret of Inner Strength*, he recalls, "Nothing came easy for me, not even being born." His birth took nearly three days and almost cost Chuck and his mother, Wilma, their lives.

The Depression was hard on all of America, but it was especially hard on Oklahoma. Like many Oklahomans, the Norrises were dirt-poor. Chuck's well-meaning but alcoholic father was always changing jobs, and by the time Chuck was fifteen he had moved thirteen times. During that time two more sons were added to the Norris family, Weiland and Aaron. Chuck rushed home from school every day to care for his younger brothers while his mother tried to make ends meet by working odd jobs. Lacking a strong male role model, Chuck spent many afternoons at Saturday matinees, where he came to idolize John Wayne and Gary Cooper, the strong and silent heroes of Westerns.

The Norrises eventually settled in Southern California in the 1950s, where Chuck had problems fitting in. He grew into a painfully shy and withdrawn teenager who never became involved in school activities because he was always helping out his family with after-school jobs. Ashamed of his poverty, he even broke up with one of his girlfriends rather than invite her home to meet his family.

DID YOU KNOW?

Chuck has one Irish and one full-blooded Cherokee Indian grandparent on each side of his family. That makes him one-fourth Irish, one-fourth Cherokee and all-American.

Things began to turn around for Chuck when he was seventeen. That's when his mother divorced his father and married a kind and generous man named George Knight. Knight went out of his way to make Chuck feel like his real son; for the first time in his life, Chuck had a male figure he could look up to. That same year Dianne Holecheck, a pretty and popular schoolmate, developed a crush on Chuck and began pursuing him. They fell in love and married right after Chuck graduated from high school in 1958.

Young and without any real prospects, Norris joined the U.S. Air Force in order to gain job experience. He was shipped to South Korea, which was still recovering from the devastation of the Korean War. Norris was stationed at Osan Air Base as an air policeman, and there was little to do during the off-hours, so he began studying judo at the base's athletic club.

One day he was wandering through the town of Osan when he heard fierce shouting coming from behind a nearby hill. As he drew closer to investigate, he saw a group of white-clad Koreans performing amazing leaps and head-high kicks. Norris had come upon a *tang soo do* class. The teacher was a stern-looking man named Jae

Chul Shin.

Norris was fascinated and soon enrolled in Master Shin's class.

In those days tang soo do training took place outdoors on hard ground, and classes were not separated into experts and beginners. Norris had no choice but to dive right in and struggle to keep up with his classmates. He trained in freezing cold and stifling heat. Some nights he returned to his quarters so sore that just lying down to sleep was sheer agony. Because of this strenuous training, Norris soon developed a sense of discipline that would carry over into every other aspect of his life. He told himself, "If I can stick with this, I can stick with anything."

Only a year after Norris began studying tang soo do, Master Shin told him that he was ready to test for his black belt in front of an examining board. The future movie star made the two-hour ride to Seoul in the dead of winter in an unheated truck. He arrived at the main *dojang* (training hall) as stiff as a board. When he got off the truck, he realized the building was open to the elements and the inside temperature was a bone-chilling eight degrees below zero.

Norris changed into his thin *gi* (training uniform) and sat in a kneeling position on one side of the hall along with the other 200 students who were testing for various ranks. He stayed in that position in the frigid cold for nearly three hours while other students demonstrated their skills under the watchful gaze of the examining board.

Finally Norris was called up and asked to demonstrate one of the basic forms, but his mind drew a blank, and he had to admit that he had forgotten the sequence. The board failed him on the spot and ordered him back to his place on the sidelines. Norris sat in misery for another hour while the rest of the students finished testing.

Disappointed, Norris returned to Osan and redoubled the intensity of his training. Three months later he tested again.

This time he visualized himself performing perfectly at the examination. That positive "mental imaging" did the trick, and Norris passed with flying colors. Even the normally unemotional Master Shin was all smiles when he presented the persistent American his black belt several weeks later.

Earning a black belt was a turning point in Norris's life. For the first time he realized he could achieve a goal as long as he set his mind to it. It was a lesson he would apply whenever he was faced with difficult circumstances.

In 1962 Norris was discharged from the air force and went to work at an aircraft company. He only planned to work at the airplane factory until he could sign on with one of Southern California's many police departments. But his dream of being a policeman would never come to

STATE OF THE ART

Chuck Norris's main art is tang soo do (way of the Chinese hand), a Korean art similar to tae kwon do. Tang soo do features among other things, a variety of spectacular kicks, including Norris's favorite technique, the spinning back kick.

pass. A few months later, his first son, Mike, was born. Norris vowed to be the good father that he never had, and he stayed at the factory.

To supplement his income, Norris began teaching tang soo do in his parents' backyard. His first two students were younger brothers Weiland and Aaron, but after several months of giving well-received demonstrations, Norris had enough students to open a small storefront dojang.

Norris soon realized he wanted to be a full-time martial arts instructor, so he quit his job and opened a second school. Still barely earning enough to support Dianne, Mike, and his newborn son, Eric, Norris entered the tournament circuit to gain some publicity for his schools. Within a year he won the California State Championship, and for the next five years he dominated the new sport of competition karate. He won every major title of the era, including back-to-back world professional karate championships in 1968 and in 1969.

Norris befriended many of the best martial artists of the era, including Bruce Lee. They trained together whenever their hectic schedules permitted, with Lee demonstrating Chinese hand techniques while Norris tried to convince Lee to include high kicks in his arsenal. Lee introduced Norris to his acquaintances in Hollywood, and Norris soon landed his first movie role, a bit part in *The Wrecking Crew* (1968), starring Dean Martin. Lee and Norris would later team on one of the great fight scenes in movie history, their battle in the Roman Colosseum in *Return of the Dragon* (1973).

Norris's star was on the rise, and soon celebrities such as Steve McQueen, Priscilla Presley, Bob Barker, and the Osmonds sought him out as a martial arts instructor. Always aware of his humble beginnings, Norris treated all of his students with courtesy, warmth, and patience, regardless of their status. By the early 1970s, Norris's following had grown to enormous proportions. He soon had a flourishing chain of schools that he operated with the

aid of talented instruct-
tors like his brother,
Aaron, and Pat
Johnson, who
later went on
to choreo-
graph *The
Karate Kid*
movies.

Despite
his new-
found success,
this was an enor-
mously difficult time
for Norris. His
brother, Weiland,
was killed in Vietnam
in 1970, a devastating loss, and one
that still haunts Norris. A few years
later, his wife, Dianne, found out that she
had cancer. Norris was afraid that he might have to face
life alone without his great love and best friend, but to his
relief Dianne recovered.

Having retired from competitive karate, Norris was cast-
ing about for a new challenge when Steve McQueen suggested that he take up acting as a second career. The soft-
spoken Oklahoman was leery at first until McQueen
reminded him of his own philosophy of conquering
objectives by careful planning, hard work, and positive
thinking. Faced with the logic of his own philosophy,
Norris picked up the gauntlet and set his mind upon
becoming a movie actor. Because of the Vietnam War,
heroism was out of fashion in the early 1970s. But swim-
ming against the tide, Norris decided that he would play a
modern version of the stoic heroes he had admired so
much as a boy.

Norris and several of his friends wrote the script for
Good Guys Wear Black. Not wanting any unearned favors

from his celebrity students, Norris looked for a producer on his own. He had exhausted almost all of his leads when he finally hooked up with a young independent movie producer. Financing was secured and the movie was shot, but that was barely the beginning of his work. Norris had to tour all over America promoting the film because the distributors refused to give it an adequate advertising budget. Nonetheless, *Good Guys Wear Black* was a success and paved the way for Norris's twenty-year-long career as one of the world's top action stars.

Today, as well as starring in movies, Norris can be seen weekly on the CBS TV show *Walker, Texas Ranger*. Norris frequently works with his brother Aaron, now a respected Hollywood director and stunt coordinator. When he is not busy teaching or working on his show, Chuck Norris finds the time to train at least three hours a day, six days a week. But more than any film or championship, he is proudest of his active involvement with many youth groups, including Kick Drugs Out of America and the Make-A-Wish Foundation, which is dedicated to granting terminally ill children their dreams.

BOW SIM MARK
(1942–)

Even as a wide-eyed girl in pigtails growing up in Canton, China, Bow Sim Mark knew that she wanted to be a martial artist. She took the first step on her long road to martial arts fame when she began studying the art of *wushu* (war arts) in elementary school. A competitive and scrappy girl even at seven, Mark's first goal in the martial arts was to be better than a second-grade classmate who just happened to be the son of a wushu master.

Mark persisted in her studies and as a teenager enrolled in a five-year professional training program at the National Wushu Institute in Canton. The curriculum included rigorous exercise, competition-oriented training, and artistic performance. She was well on her way to becoming a full-time martial artist, despite traditional Chinese attitudes that discouraged women from pursuing martial arts for fear that they might develop a reputation for "toughness" and lose any chance of finding a husband.

Upon completing her studies at the institute in 1962, Mark became a private student of Fu Wing Fay, one of the most noted masters in all of China. Master Fu was a stern teacher who pushed Mark even harder than he pushed his male students. As Mark later recalled, the very first thing Master Fu told his young pupil was, "Forget everything you have already learned; now you have to learn the right way."

Under Fu Wing Fay's tutelage, Mark mastered the straight Chinese sword and the "internal" arts of *t'ai chi ch'uan* (supreme ultimate fist) and *pa kua chang* (eight trigrams boxing). The "internal" arts were ideal for the petite Mark because they stressed balance, timing, and redirection of force rather than brute strength.

Mark excelled under Master Fu's watchful eye and eventually became one of his assistant instructors. After ten

STATE OF THE ART

Wushu is the official martial art of modern China. It can be used for self-defense, exercise, competition, and artistic performance. Wushu comprises many traditional Chinese martial arts styles.

Bow Sim Mark is known for her expertise in the "soft" aspects of wushu, such as the arts of t'ai chi ch'uan and pa kua chang (pronounced *ba gwa*). The "internal" arts rely on calmness, proper body mechanics, and timing rather than on the speed or physical strength of the "hard" or "external" styles. Although the "external" styles are best practiced by the young and fit, "internal" mastery remains even in old age.

years of concentrated study, Master Fu gave Mark the highest possible praise when he awarded her a scroll that declared, "This is a follower who has mastered all I can teach."

In 1973 Mark relocated to Hong Kong along with her husband and two young children. Hong Kong is a bustling city with a very rough side, and Mark saw the need for women to learn martial arts as a means of self-defense. Acting on that belief, she opened the first women's martial arts school in the city. Another teacher at the school was Fu Wing Fay's wife, Ho Ga-Hsin.

In addition to her role as the school's chief instructor, Mark also performed in a classical Chinese opera troupe. More than just a martial artist, she proved to be an excellent singer and actress. Today, she still champions the incorporation of martial arts into theater, working with such prestigious organizations as Harvard University's American Repertory Theater.

In 1975 Mark was invited to tour the United States, where she gave critically acclaimed wushu performances nationwide. On that tour she fell in love with America and the following year moved her family to Boston, Massachusetts. In Boston she opened the first wushu school in the United States, the Chinese Wushu Research Institute. The Institute has since produced many talented students, some of whom have even won medals in competitions in mainland China.

Bow Sim Mark is known as a patient and inspirational teacher who pushes all of her students to their limits without resorting to harsh or demoralizing methods.

Even when her students don't achieve true mastery she helps them on the road to "discipline, calmness, and quiet power." Mark believes that determination is more important than natural physical aptitude. "All that I really ask of my students," she says, "is that they keep trying."

Recognized as one of the premier martial arts teachers in the world, Bow Sim Mark was named *Black Belt* magazine's 1996 Instructor of the Year and *Inside Kung-Fu* magazine's Woman of the Year in 1994 and 1996. She remains dedicated to showing the world the power and beauty of wushu through countless exhibitions, seminars, and international competitions.

DID YOU KNOW?

Martial arts talent runs in Bow Sim Mark's family. Her daughter, Chi Ching Yen, has won numerous medals in international competition, while her son, Donnie Yen, is a major movie and TV star in Hong Kong, appearing in *Dragon Inn*, *Once Upon a Time in China II*, *Iron Monkey*, and *Fists of Fury*.

MASUTATSU "MAS" OYAMA
(1923–1994)

Imagine yourself
traveling back in
time to 1951. You are
walking in the forested mountains south of
Tokyo, Japan. The sun is just rising; morning mists hang
over the trees, and the air is so cold that you can see your
breath.

As you move through the woods you hear the crash of
a small waterfall spilling over the cliffs ahead. Pushing
your way through thick brush and low-hanging branches,
the waterfall comes into view and you see a man sitting
beneath the spray. You wouldn't dare stick even a hand in
the painfully cold water, but the man just sits there as
gallons of the stuff pour over him. He doesn't move. He
doesn't flinch. He doesn't scream in agony. All he does is
sit there, eyes closed, meditating.

You shiver and think the man must be crazy.

Masutatsu "Mas" Oyama wasn't crazy. He was driven.

For nearly three years he lived alone in the mountain
forests, practicing for up to twelve hours a day and honing his karate skills to near perfection. His relentless train-

ing regimen included breaking river stones with his bare hands to toughen his knuckles and kicking tree trunks to toughen his legs (don't try this at home!). To increase his leaping ability and stamina, Oyama would jump for hours over the tangled undergrowth.

But he wasn't content with just training his body. Oyama also studied many classic texts on martial arts, Zen Buddhism, and philosophy, such as *The Book of Five Rings* by the great samurai swordsman Miyamoto Musashi.

What drove Oyama? What made him leave the comforts of civilization for the rigors of the untamed Japanese wilderness?

Born Yee Hyung in Kimje, Korea, the young boy studied Chinese and Korean martial arts from the age of nine. Yee Hyung dreamed of becoming a fighter pilot, so his parents scraped together enough money to send him to a military academy in Japan when he was fifteen. There he learned karate, judo, and boxing. But he wasn't happy.

Nearly thirty years before Yee Hyung came to Japan, the Japanese had conquered Korea. As many conquerors have throughout history, the Japanese treated the countries they invaded harshly. Korea was no exception. The people were forced to work for the Japanese, and they lived under military rule.

In Japan, Yee Hyung was scorned by his classmates because of his Korean ancestry and was eventually forced to leave the school. Taking a Japanese name, Masutatsu Oyama, he moved to Tokyo, Japan's capital, where he trained in Shotokan karate. Oyama's teacher was Gichin Funakoshi, the great Okinawan master who had intro-

STATE OF THE ART

Kyokushinkai karate is an extremely rugged style that features unprotected full-contact sparring to test stamina, technique, and courage. Students also practice board breaking and learn Zen meditation techniques to improve mental focus. Most karate styles are hard and linear, but kyokushinkai also incorporates many softer, circular movements.

duced karate to Japan more than a decade earlier.

When Japan attacked Pearl Harbor, Hawaii, in 1941, triggering war with the United States, Oyama was drafted into Japan's Imperial Army and assigned to a special unit that trained spies and commandos. Despite his earlier experiences at the military academy, he had become a Japanese patriot who, if called upon, would give his life for the island nation.

After Japan surrendered to the Allies in 1945, Oyama studied with So Nei Chu, a master of Okinawan *goju-ryu* karate. Master So saw that Oyama was despondent over Japan's defeat. He suggested that Oyama go into the wilderness to strengthen his mind and body.

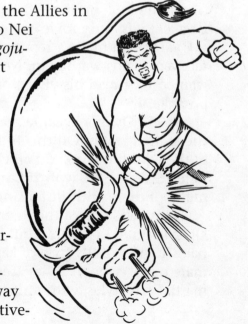

That's why Oyama jour-neyed to the mountains to break rocks, kick trees, and meditate under ice-cold water-falls.

Upon his return to civiliza-tion, Oyama searched for a way to prove the power and effectiveness of his karate both to himself and to the world at large. Walking by a slaughterhouse one afternoon, he found his answer: He would fight bulls marked for slaughter.

Oyama's first fight with a bull must have been quite a show. As the slaughterhouse workers watched, Oyama was chased out of the stock-yard by an angry bull. Even Oyama had to admit that he had failed. But he didn't give up. In his next attempt, Oyama stunned a bull with a single blow to its forehead and then sheared off one of its horns with a knife-hand strike.

DID YOU KNOW?

When Oyama gave a demonstration in Mexico in 1957, one particularly ornery bull managed to gore him. Oyama barely managed to fend off the beast's next attack and snap off its horns. He spent the next six months recovering from wounds that would have killed most other men.

Fighting bulls became Mas Oyama's claim to fame. In his life he took on more than fifty bulls, often in front of large crowds and movie cameras.

Oyama had made a reputation for himself in rapidly recovering postwar Japan. Now he had a new goal. He wanted to spread his vision of karate as far and wide as possible.

In 1952 Oyama became the first karate master to visit the United States. On this tour and on visits to other parts of the world, he took on all challengers, regardless of their fighting styles. He won 270 matches without a loss—many of them with just a single blow.

Oyama was one of the first great karate showmen, the "P. T. Barnum of karate," but he had the skills to match his flair. He named his style of karate the *kyokushinkai* or "ulti-mate truth" school. Today it is one of the most popular martial arts styles, with millions of members worldwide.

FILEMON "MOMOY" DE LA CUESTA CANETE

(1904–1995)

Some martial arts masters achieve enormous fame and fortune in their own lifetimes. Others are "masters' masters," receiving acclaim largely from their peers, legends only to the experts. One such man is Filemon "Momoy" Canete, master of the Philippine art of *eskrima* (from the Spanish word for fencing).

Canete was a native of Cebu Island in the central Philippines. Cebu was claimed for Spain in the early sixteenth century by Ferdinand Magellan, the first man to sail around the world. According to legend, Magellan was killed in battle by the chieftain Lapu-Lapu of nearby Mactan Island, who was a talented swordsman. Thus the Cebu region has always been known for the skill of its *eskrimadors* (eskrima practitioners).

Thousands of Spanish conquistadors would invade the Philippines within a few short years of Magellan's death, subjugating most of the people except for the fiercely independent Muslim tribes on the southern island of Mindanao. The native fighting arts of the islands were banned by the Spanish on penalty of death. For more

than 300 years all eskrima training had to take place in
secret or be disguised as dance.

Spain lost the Philippines to the United States in the
Spanish-American War of 1898. Momoy Canete was born
six years later in one of the toughest neighborhoods in
Cebu City. Canete began to study eskrima in his early
teens. His teacher was Teodoro Saveedra, and his early
training emphasized a close-quarter stick fighting method
called *tapi-tapi*, named after the use of the free or non-
weapon hand to check and control the opponent's
weapon.

By the time Canete was twenty-four, he was already a
full instructor. Four years later in 1932, he and his seven
brothers, Eulogio, Tirsio, Rufino, Florentino, Andres,
Silvestre, and Ciriaco (Cacoy), formed their own martial
arts club. They named it the Doce Pares Society after a
select group of warriors who served the Holy Roman
Emperor Charlemagne (A.D. 768–814).

The Doce Pares Society was a hotbed of martial arts
activity. Many notable fighters and masters passed
through the club, stopping to work out or cross-train with
the Canete brothers. The club soon became a laboratory,
where Momoy developed and refined his own brand of
eskrima. He emphasized subtly evasive footwork and pow-

erful long-range strikes with a thirty-three-inch stick. He also favored training with a wooden dagger in the off hand, usually reserving it for follow-ups to the sweeping stick strikes.

The Canetes were not afraid to borrow from many sources. New weapons that they incorporated into their style included knives, spears, the short staff, and the *cadan*, a metal chain. They even learned to use the bullwhip from a wild-animal trainer.

When Japan invaded the Philippines during World War II, many eskrimadors joined special units to fight for their homeland. Their close-combat skills proved excellent in jungle warfare. Momoy Canete chose to help out his countrymen by taking to the mountains with the resistance movement and serving as a healer.

Always a devout Catholic, Canete had developed a reputation as a man with strong spiritual powers. He had a litany of prayers that he used to heal the sick, exorcise evil spirits, and demoralize opponents. In one amusing incident, a small boy jammed a tamarind seed so far up his nose that no one could remove it;

DID YOU KNOW?

The Cebu region in the Philippines is famous for its singers and musicians, and Momoy Canete was known as an exceptionally gifted guitarist, singer, and songwriter in addition to his expertise in the martial arts. Some of his students believed that his skills at creating forms and training drills, as well as his superb sense of rhythm and timing, were a result of his innate musical talent.

STATE OF THE ART

Also referred to as *kali*, or *arnis de mano*, eskrima is the chief fighting art of the Philippine Islands. It features a wide variety of weapons, but the most common are swords and wooden sticks of varying lengths. Momoy Canete's specialty was a form called *espada y daga*, which uses a long stick or blade in one hand and a straight dagger in the other, a form influenced by the rapier and dagger fencing techniques the Spanish invaders brought to the Philippines at the end of the sixteenth century.

Canete only had to recite some *palabras* (power words), and the seed dropped right out. Even if his abilities were not mystical in origin, they proved to be very effective in focusing mental and physical energy in emergencies, like the mantras (incantations) that have been used for thousands of years in India.

After the war Canete returned to Cebu City, where he continued to teach and refine his eskrima. His younger brother, Cacoy, and other members of the Doce Pares Society became instrumental in popularizing eskrima in the United States and the rest of the world. The "grand old man" of eskrima, Momoy remained in the background, content to refine his art.

Momoy Canete taught small and informal eskrima groups in his backyard, and over the years skilled eskrimadors the world over began to make the pilgrimage to see the Grandmaster of Cebu. A true eskrima master, Momoy trained up to his death in 1995 at age ninety-one. His students recall Canete as a small and physically unimpressive man who seemed to turn into a giant when facing his opponent in battle. With his powerful gaze and perfect posture, he resembled an ancient warrior chieftain, glowing with the spirit of combat.

MORE MARTIAL ARTS MASTERS

YIP MAN (?–1972): A grandmaster of wing chun kung fu, Yip Man was one of the best martial artists in Hong Kong. He is most famous as Bruce Lee's teacher.

LILY LAU (1947–   ): The only woman kung fu grandmaster alive today, her eagle claw system is famous for its seizing and grappling attacks. Lau inherited leadership of the eagle claw system when her father passed away, despite the fact that she was only seventeen.

ED PARKER (1931–1990): A Hawaiian who introduced kenpo karate to the American mainland, Parker modernized and Americanized the art by using English-language terms and creating a very scientific and systematic lesson plan. He was one of the first martial artists to work in Hollywood, and he taught many famous students, including William Shatner and Elvis Presley. Parker also choreographed and performed fight scenes for the silver screen. Among his greatest accomplishment was the Long Beach Internationals, the most prestigious martial arts tournament in North America.

Ed Parker

DANIEL INOSANTO (1936–   ): Bruce Lee's number-one student, Inosanto is the man most responsible for keeping jeet kune do alive. Equally important is his role in introducing the martial arts of the Philippines and other Southeast Asian countries to the American public.

BENNY "THE JET" URQUIDEZ (1952–   ): Benny Urquidez is probably the best kickboxer alive, having held an undefeated record of fifty-eight wins and no losses for more than twenty years.

STEVEN SEAGAL (1952–   ): The enigmatic and often-controversial action movie star has taken aikido back to its combat roots, both on-screen and at his traditional-style dojos.

LOUIS VIGNERON (1827–1871): The greatest champion of savate, a high-kicking French martial art, Vigneron was also a champion weightlifter and a circus strongman. He was nicknamed the "Human Cannon" for his most famous stunt, which involved holding a 440-pound cannon on his shoulders and firing it without any support.

"JUDO" GENE LEBELL (1932–   ): Also known as the "Grappling Master," LeBell won back-to-back national judo championships in 1954 and 1955 before becoming a professional wrestler. Many other prominent martial artists, including Chuck Norris, Benny Uriquidez, and Bruce Lee have turned to him for tips on the art of grappling.

BILL "SUPERFOOT" WALLACE (1945–   ): Wallace earned the nickname "Superfoot" because of his lightning-fast kicks. He was one of the dominant kickboxers of the 1970s and 1980s, finishing with a record of twenty-one wins and no losses.

JEAN-CLAUDE VAN DAMME (1961–   ): Laugh at his thick Belgian accent if you must, but Van Damme has proven to be one of the most dynamic and exciting screen martial artists since the heyday of Bruce Lee.

DR. MAUNG GYI (1933–?): A former member of the elite Gurkha regiments of the British Army, Dr. Gyi fought behind enemy lines in World War II, Korea, and Vietnam. He introduced the Burmese art of *bando* to the United States in 1960, which includes extensive weapons training and a kickboxing element similar to Thai boxing.

MANOEL DOS REIS MACHADO AKA **MESTRE BIMBA (1899–1974):** Mestre Bimba was a master of the Brazilian art of *capoeira*. Developed by African slaves, the art is performed to live musical accompaniment and has elements of real combat, dance, and gamesmanship. Capoeira was banned for more than a century by the Brazilian government until Mestre Bimba opened the first public academy in the 1930s.

Photo courtesey of Surachai Sirisute

SURACHAI "CHAI" SIRISUTE (?–?): Born in Bangkok, Thailand, Chai Sirisute, commonly referred to as Master Chai, was one of the great champions of muay Thai, or Thai boxing. He introduced the art to the United States in 1968

Surachai Sirisute

and has gone on to establish associations around the world.

WILLIAM K.S. "THUNDERBOLT" CHOW (1913–1987): Hawaiian-born Chow was a kenpo master renowned for his irascible temperament and awesome skills. His famous students include Ed Parker; Adriano Emperado, co-founder of Kajukenbo; and Sam Kuoha, head of the kara-ho kempo system.

ROBERT KOGA (?–   ): A veteran of the Los Angeles Police Department, Bob Koga is a master of judo, jujutsu, and aikido. For more than twenty years he has been the foremost police self-defense instructor in the country. He is also the inventor of the Koga police baton, an updated and highly refined version of the traditional police billy club.

GLOSSARY

Boldfaced words in the definitions are also glossary terms.

Aikido A Japanese martial art that stresses the redirection of the opponent's force.

Bokken A heavy wooden practice sword used in **kenjutsu**.

Chinese or **Peking Opera** A traditional form of Chinese theater that combines acrobatics, singing, and the martial arts.

Dan The upper or black belt ranks of a martial art. Note that having a black belt does *not* mean that you are automatically a master. In Asia, the black belt simply means that a student has mastered the basics and is ready to begin studying the advanced aspects of his or her art.

Dojang The Korean term for training hall.

Dojo The Japanese word for training hall.

Eskrima Also known as *kali* or *armis de mano*, eskrima is the fighting art of the Philippine Islands that features extensive weapons training, as well as empty-hand techniques.

Forms Martial arts techniques that are arranged in present sequences in order to make them easier to learn and apply.

Gi The pajama-like uniform first used in **judo** and now used in many different martial arts. Most styles favor black or white uniforms.

Internal vs. External *Internal* or "soft" martial arts concentrate on developing timing and proper body mechanics over physical speed and strength. The most famous internal styles include **aikido**, pakua, and t'ai chi. Masters of the internal arts are capable of delivering incredibly powerful blows with no visible effort.

External or "hard" arts such as **tae kwon do** and kickboxing are not necessarily inferior to the interior arts. The external systems are usually much easier to learn and apply in combat situations. Most martial arts combine both aspects and are not just "external" or "internal."

Judo The first of the modern martial arts, judo emphasizes throws and grappling techniques.

Jujutsu The forerunner to judo, jujutsu was the martial art of the samurai warriors of feudal Japan.

Jutsu vs. Do *Jutsu* is a Japanese word meaning "art"; *do* means "way." Jutsu martial arts are mostly combat-oriented, whereas the do systems evolved from the older jutsu forms and focus on physical, mental, and spiritual self-improvement. For example, the no-holds-barred fighting of **ju*jutsu*** gave rise to modern Kodakan **ju*do***.

Karate An Okinawan art known for its powerful punches and kicks.

Kata The Japanese term for forms.

Katana The long, curved sword used by the **samurai**. It was worn along with the short **wakizashi**.

Kenjutsu Traditional Japanese swordmanship.

Kiai A shout that is used in many martial arts to focus one's efforts. A powerful kiai can make opponents hesitate or sometimes even temporarily stun them.

Kwoon The Chinese term for martial arts school.

Muay Thai The national sport of Thailand, muay Thai is an aggressive martial art known for its close-quarter knee and elbow strikes, in addition to traditional punching and kicking techniques.

Samurai A member of the special warrior class of feudal Japan, similar to the knights of medieval Europe.

Shogun A line of military leaders who ruled Japan until 1868.

Tae kwon do A spectacular kicking art that hails from Korea.

Tang soo do A close cousin of **tae kwon do** that also features a wide variety of spectacular kicks.

Wakizashi The short sword of feudal Japan. When worn with the **katana**, it was a sign of rank of the warrior and noble classes.

Wushu The official martial art of the People's Republic of China.

INDEX